AF413516

Too Far Too Deep

TOO FAR
TOO DEEP

SHANTHA

Notion Press

Old No. 38, New No. 6

McNichols Road, Chetpet

Chennai - 600 031

First Published by Notion Press 2015

Copyright © Shantha 2015

All Rights Reserved.

ISBN:

Paperback 978-93-5206-389-5

Hardcase 979-8-89498-082-9

Most writing is inspired, and something was lit in me
when I wrote these. As I explore my own horizons
of feeling I discover that, deep underneath all layers
is a core of happiness which is to be experienced.
Kochi, a seeker par-excellence, lit my lamp when
I was in utter darkness.

CONTENTS

Contents

INNER GARMENTS

The inner garments
I found them wanting for wear
Until the inner merged with the outer.

These inner garments
United me with mine
I decked my hair real fine
And let gold touch me as thine.

These inner garments soft
Made hardness come forth
Happiness dissolved in sadness
Tears brought a smile.

These inner garments Oh!
Melted my ego
As I saw myself go.

NAME

If I had a new name
A brand new name
An enticing attractive new name
An inviting feminine sexual name.

If only I had a new name
An unused, untouched name
Purity, simplicity of a name
Never re-used will be my new name.

Will I love my new name
Will it give me fame
Will the world be seen as new?
Or as only from new frames.

This new name without meaning
Will it be a beginning
Will it change the inner and enlighten?
If only I had a new name.

RUNNER

I told her to be smart
I told her to smile
I told her she is to run
For running will take her far.

But I play cricket, she said
For I can do the square cut like nobody else;
I waited for her to run
For running I knew will take her far.

But she brought home a ball
Soccer is the newest fad of all
I shall use my body to fight the ball
While I urged her……………..

Running will take you far.

FRIEND

A friend is to be a foe
Not for beauty or protection
As the pairing of thorn and rose
But, as person for them to you know.

Light a flame for her love
The warmth attracts but heat burns
Be the breeze that moves the flame
The deep dark inside of a burning flame.

As the yellow moon rises
And the cool flame bloweth
Fire of love and kindness kindles

Friend and foe become oneth.

EMOTIONS

They were there
In some depth they were
Without manifestations though they were.

They would flower
When I became learned
Knowledge will be their growth
In the right season they will come forth.

I flowered with gusto without fruit
They surfaced not but I grew
In pristine solitude I dug roots
Further lost them I, they said it was youth.

Feelings were there
So it happened one day
They came forth urging me to give way.

Emotions exposed I kept pace
With and without I raced
I win you win and this shall be the way.

NIGHTINGALE

Had I wings I would have flown
It is that close but fly I cannot
I heard the bird call but take me she could not.

Measured the distance one foot at a time
It is time but time flies
Were my wings clipped and parents lost?

Maybe tomorrow when tomorrow comes
The feet have a mind of their own
And destinations have a name.

It matters not if only I could fly
For tomorrow never dies
Nightingales do not lie.

THE FACE

Do I search for his face
Do I search for his house
Amongst thousands do I search.

By the side of the vast calm river
Under the rocks on the river front
Haunted by the stories.

Gave up the search I did
Time will come when it will
The face of my mind's eye
Cometh into its dwelling.

But room there is not here
Did I want or was it always near.
This I cannot tell; I will share
That dreams I will not fear.

CHRISTMAS LIFE

Life is precious
Life is complex
Life is time.

Life is wheels within wheels
Moving towards one another
Or opposed to the other.

Like wheels embedded together
Bound, hammered to bodies
Moving yet inevitably, inexplicably.

The wheels see the guiding light
That far lit spot of sun
Urging silently to come forth.

Flesh, time and wheel merge into the light
Complexity dissolves with crushing pain
But life exists without the blood, speech and sight.

Life is beyond birth, rebirth, loving
Pain, pleasure, passion all fleeting
Reach for your light before the ending.

GURU

A guru a guide I became
Woman or girl as I was borne
Without a worldly guide or inner shine
From a mother who had some aim.

I did not become her;
When I was led astray
She came to me in another way
The rainbows, the maddening rain held my sway.

Till that day everything gave way
Nothing remained that was gay
I held out my hand for the one flower
Guru, the giver and music filled me in every way…

DANCE

Cards have to be played right
Math is to be conquered
Music mastered
Dance not before you might.

My shoes are worn and my feet ache
I mend them till they take
From hot sand to freezing snow
What is normal will I ever know?

The shining new pair
Under the gown was there
It was given to all, wear wear
I then danced without a care.

BLUE

The lightness in the blue sky
Grabbing it, my hands try
I look down, in the blue sea is the same sky.

Sky's blue is the right amount of blue
Sun making the blue lighter
My blue shoes hold tighter
Go not yet because the blue will fade.

It gets deeper, as the sun leaves its bluer
With the moon rising it is fearfully darker
The blue is gone, the black I want not ever.

My skirt of all colours flows
The blue dancing flowers in it radiate
My moist blue eyes in the mirror gaze
I feel the blue shoes gathering gait.

Go not dear, just wait

The vast sea is beginning to rise

In comes the blue sky in your own trait!!

FLYING

Is this because of growing
In flight he was alone dreaming
Left someone behind longing.

He left to grab the stars
Those grades were calling
The four pointers for vanity sake gaining.

She looks for him again
In those very spots
Gone are the sounds and commanding.

Scattered lives only remaining.

THE LYCHEE TREE

I can never be free
The child lost its freedom
In steps with growth of the lychee tree.

The fruit it bore were too high
To reach it was a hard try
The scratches and cuts made her cry.

While sitting in the jeep she reached
Where her lychee tree she took sight
Grabbed one fruit but many fell on wayside.

Sitting with one fruit in hand
Brooding on those that lay crushed
Looking behind her desires got subdued.

What fell also remained bound
What grew still shaded the ground
The air she breathed caused the leaves to rustle.

Maybe Indeed I was Free.

MONKEY DANCE

Monkey dance of the eons
Flat footed open mouth hunched bodies
Laughed loud and beat their breasts
That face, those eyes, yes an icon.

When did those feet shrink tiny
Who tied them to make them puny
The tired bodies that now walk straight
With dainty feet forming picture so funny.

The clothes gave the shape
Feet half raised to tap
Breast squeezed so hard as not to beat
Faces beautiful, lips coloured but rhythm of defeat.

Sit they gaping and thinking of the bygone
Forgetting their dance and their own ways
Rise they might when given the space
Monkeys then will dance joyous and gay.

TRAVELS

Bring different changes journey can
Many roads, many a travels through world's dens
Core is only changeless say all great men.

Like digging in earth mines to find
The yellow streaks golden and divine
Or walking in muddied and infested waters
Sieving through with fingers for earthly matters.

Comes to some a large diamond
This gem too had its travels
From core to light when it came
Brought awareness, such joy, so humane.

CREATOR

It is creators creation
Living is just a demonstration
Great thoughts of sophistication
Strength of action to world bring sensations.

Mind evolved to increased complexity
Action through challenge brought dexterity
Child of creator created variety
It is in us that creator grows to immortality.

TO A BETTER PLACE

You saw the change that changed you
New sensations besieged you
With emotions overwhelming you drowned
Not peace, not power your ground.

Sun rose you not from slumber
Moon rose gave a night no calmer
Deep stirrings made soul darker
Fighter was borne to make a survivor.

Said you if all is mine and all illusion
I can throw all without devastation
Long you thought for your vision
Started then your journey amongst the million.

A road so special free of care
Pure thoughts that no pain dare
Flowers under your feet everywhere
A stumble here a stumble there.

Mattered no more no where.

BRIGHT CASTLE

Its a way of no way
Its freedom in a way
Loneness comes in all colours
Like gusty winds full of power.

The castle grew out of white clouds
Rain and wild winds howling loud
Tensions filled the air with longing
Desire on every corner that I bowed.

Fifteen thousand books hide the desire
I looked inside every cover for fire
I read the lines and between the lines
Mysterious energy I need is only for hire.

For it is not over
A story still being written for her
A happy ending always for the other
Here are burnt books, broken glass and dead lover.

If books can talk and walls can laugh
Rebuild I can't still this castle of life
Towers in the cloud reaching for the star
Not for me, I cannot with myself war.

No day, no dawn, no sunshine
I lost all and still found one
The self, the I, the thought of divine
In this castle new pain is still; feelings fine.

The walk of the tired soles
Burnt skin ready for coal
Matters not freedom part or whole
Fools come to live where living need to be consoled.

CLIFF ROCKS

Hard as only hardness knows
In my hand it bruises
I notice the blister and nicks
Softness is softer with each grip.

But hardness is as is!

The rocks too are lost
Long back were they the haughty soldier
The sea kept them in her moist palm
Drenched, washed and nourished with her life.

Sun and rain cost their stony luster
Earthly richness melted in force of water
Shapes and sharpness blown with time
But hardness, wind rain or cloud did not gain.

Hardness remained for another harness.

FEAR

The clasp of the wrist
In late morning mist
A hundred steps more
You would have seen the turns and twists.

Before the hold of confusion
Your path had direction
You knew it was free of false exultation
And hidden damnation.

You planted the frailing footsteps
Empty silent and firm
You heard the echo of anonymous steps
When your own succumbed to patient
submissiveness.

NEW LOVE

Summer heat bearing down
In sweat, toil and laser rays
I search for new love in new ways.

I need love to beat the heat
Will fight till my own defeat
Open my heart in wild beat.

Quench my thirst with your nectar
Sullied I fall in cave of surrender
It was cool, the summer cool of forever.

Come sweet love in groves to wander!

ZARI GOWN

I look straight on
Catching the sight of the eons
Changes that I felt and understood
Much more that unchanging continues.

Slowing down I let things pass
In unending streams they rush
A simple gesture but aside I was cast
As if drifting in ocean vast.

All things golden are found
In a sunny boulevard of town
Trinklets, tingling bells and zari gown
I was draped in living, shimmering form.

A circular whirlpool that pulls you down
Bringing you to the changeless you recrown.

DEATH IN AN EARTHQUAKE

What's luck got to do with it
Earth's crack and destruction ever brings new dawn
Man-created fire defies gravity in ways unknown.

Here today gone tomorrow
That's for seasons and ground furrows
For me the unsown grows and leaves an afterglow.

I muted the fire of the senses
With flute, piano and more sounds of within
Navigating to a bottomless ocean of closeness.

Sounds are clearer in this ocean
Fire gives heat to thriving life in water
Corals, flora, fauna against a glassy sheen.

Recreate a new world with.

IN MY TAPESTRY

If you endure know why
Five fingers of five senses
Hold and work together for your joy
Alone, separated, even paired they lie.

Conflicting signals fill your heritage
Wonderful sights boxed in memories
Blindness alongside grew in audacity
It took but a gentle nudge of brutality.

The infant is the only remaining sign of sanity
Oh precious life in my tapestry
The fruit of my flavours and vitality
Be it there alone for posterity.

I bow and the pass the same to all
Sit into this picture of commonality!

SMALL CELL

Where did I hear life is precious?
Whose life is it anyway?
The source is but one.

Maybe size matters after all
Life is there in big and small
Deep unto to the invisible walls.

Through the barrier of seeing and feel
There exists the smallest of being
Crushed unknowing but living.

This is the one precious of calling
Wholesome yet divisive
Source of all is in hiding.

Its nectar of honey yellow deeply unifying.

LOST IN CLOUDS

For a while the senses were shut
In the thunder, rumbling and rain
Overpowering all of my brain
The very fluid froze in my insides in every vein.

It was the common sound of activity that arose
The clapping and chatter that did restore
A feeling of being and belonging as it were
A heightened awareness of my living.

Matter and manifestations abound
Clouds lighting up with the sun rays
White light dancing in skyways
Ultimately to this surrender I awoke.

THE GOLD MEDAL

NO NO! He said but twice in his life
It took him away from place of strife.

I ran around the field searching
For him who understood what I had been saying.

But he had ended his journey at the very top
The icy cold place which in past had him stop.

Challenge is compelling in sport
Most fall in their journey to one spot.

Reconcile in peace cast in gold
Search on for there isn't just one single truth.

In control, in withdrawl and inner silence
There lurks a fountain source of guidance.

Make a mirror of this substance
Look in it for energy for your existence.

Life is previous but living is its consequence
You can with just a mirror for reverence!!

SNOW

I had my first sighting of snow
It was not icy cold
There it lay crushed by every sole.

On the roads and pavements
Even on the well-trimmed grass
In the gardens it lay alongside winter blooms.

My favourite river was not spared
On its moored canoes they were
Forming small ice mountains they floated.

The snow in its softness does not kill
It is waters that heavens conceal
At will you can merry or simply chill.

The message is just one, LIVE TO YOUR FILL.

THE WAR BRIDE

The adornments on the body
Were meant as armaments
The gold skirt to shirk the arrows
Could open with the gentlest touch.

The long triple gold chain was showy
Guarding her heart so kindly
The dye was cast for some revelery
As night fell she crept away for solitary.

A long search among the houses
Brought her to one with a flag post
Inside were no grooms but men of duty
Each she asked for their identity.

Replies came but no answers
Doubts appeared on her face as changing colours
For her knight she was the shining armour
All was lost as was he in her.

She rose as war-bride in a slow firm stride.

DUST BEYOND YOUR CITY

I needed my durbin to see you
I believe they call it lens
It magnifies and expands all in sight
Brings them closer when all else fails.

It had looked dusty through my naked eyes
The far off city where you reside
Furious dust storms of dry desert
Come to lay claim in disguise.

For it is not desert where you are
Plants, orchids, nasturtiums delight
Streams of flowing water you so love
Rocky sit outs that you lounge at night.

Yet each morning when I see the dust
Lying silent and tranquil
In perfect union with dew drops
All promises and vows are fulfilled.

DESIRE

Stars twinkle like diamonds
My heart flutters without thought
My skin tingles with feelings
My throat is parched for words.

Diamonds are real, stars too
Thoughts matter of feelings few
Goad the desires everyday anew
I rather walk on early morning dew.

THE STICKS

A wanderer amongst men
A near naked heedless child
Looking around with a mission
Pure of vision, looking to beyond.

A lone whiteness seen through the mist
Body wreathed in early blue morn
Having fallen in pieces and torn
Yet ready to rise in ernest, not forlorn.

The sticks will warm his cave
Cared he not for what living gave
The blood will melt and fire save
It keeps coming to breath take.

The trees that gave the sticks
The mountains with hollow bellies
The caves that ensconsed the fire
His blood, body and soul are ALL life's mire.

BRAHMAKUMARI

She took out my eyes with her fingers
They left me and joined to her
Slowly through cycles of fire and water they passed
To merge into her unknown mind and cast.

Her beauty and purity truly unsurpassed
In one being set with masterly craft
Leaving an active past to redraft
She gave herself a new birth unabashed.

I lost some bit of me in her
Will she know that now my vision is a blur?
Yet there is no wrath to incur
Rather I wait to see her starry grandeur.

Touching the skies with her silvery white
As if she were in herself the alpine fir.

END OF SUNRISE

Where the end is found
The sun rises red
Beautiful large radiant round.

You feel the smile on its face
Your lips touch the sun surface
Its cool but it burns.

You recoil and smile at its beauty
When you look around
Mountains beautiful surround.

I reach out again to the rising sun
Want of warmth for I miss
Overwhelmed with joy again I kiss
Is this the end that I wish?

MYSELF

You are blind
You are without feeling
You are light;
But fright is your killing.

You are love
You are softness
A bit of yourself you find in singing
Yet; fright is your killing.

You are amazing
Beauty of heart is for keeping
Mind of yours is amazing
Even so; fright is all killing.

You are seeing
Your companionship is for enjoying
Your hands are for holding
Ever though; fright is killing.

Your mind is for giving
A deeper mind for learning
Your words have meaning
Forever though; fright is killing.

Your heart is small
Your soul very small too
Your presence is invisible
Even in the smallness; fright is killing.

God sent you family
Blessed you with birthing
Your wealth is mind-boggling
Fright; Oh this fright is killing.

UNION

By the banks of Ganga
Lure the temples of Shiva
Running at its edge
Reflecting the colours of Kali.

He lived there in panchavati
Sat on the ghats, took boat into the river
Loving her as son, loving her as a lover.

They sang and laughed
In devotion to Shiva
Way to Kailash uphill as it was,
Stopped not the priest for Kali at his side was.

Pray for strength and endurance
Pray with love not for love,
True devotee of Kali become.

THERAPY

Awkward silences I foresaw not
Nor the tiptoeing steps
They speak softly and in intimacy
My heart cried he belongs to me.

The gentle conversations continued
The words not reaching me
My strained ears know not if it was them or me
The same deviousness swallowed him.

My heart cried where is me and mine?
I consoled me this is not the time
Put away pain, it is only ego
Gather your humility to let go.

What's mine will sure come to me
But the whispers disturb
Today's closeness like a glass curtain is
Where are the walls of black scribble which haunt me?

He dug out eyes wherever he saw
Today is yesterday's ghost in their lives
The spirit that drove which death defied
Giving life, today lifeless in core survives.

QUESTION

Can the heart be torn to pieces?
The heart can be torn to pieces
If sounds and cries of pain come not from the heart
IF wounds can be healed without blood of the heart.

Blind gets sight and girl finds her teacher
Why not then heal the gentle heart of this preacher
Give him love but remain not a fighter
Use his journey's end to take your life higher.

He shows the miracle, says no to food
Sees your dreams as he sees his pasthood
Your parent, your child, he is all to your wish
His BOUND feet you worship…………………..

KNOW IT NOT AS BLISS.

MEMORIES

All things will pass
I knew this from the start
Holding to moments of now fast
Separate I could not from my own part.

It needs two to play bat and ball
Two face to face to talk
Like the ground beneath to run on
Time binds the inside to outside all.

Imprints of emotions form thought
Routine acts only nought
Great winners are born of passion
Games only lost by anger and tension.

I stay or leave it's my will

I walk or run or stay still

Same as asking why on Kailash is Shiv?

She will not let you touch her feet
Nor can her eyes at level meet
Body covered in stiff cloth you may greet.

DIVINITY, godliness her mindful TREAT.

BLOOM

So many flowers in all colours
Their charm is fragrance and form
I smelt each one in turn
For soon it will be time to mourn.

Running helter skelter to touch
Searching for that which was unknown
Hidden to the world hardly grown
Crushed to near death by its very own.

There was one soft and tender
Born on a long stalk slender
Folded on to itself in shyness
Deep I put my finger to find its center.

No empty cove or secrets hidden
Beauty which comes forth of sudden
Come it today or tomorrow
Life is too fragile for sorrow.

EXIT

I heard him eyes wide
My ears hurt he spoke so loud
HE HAD BEEN SENT ESPECIALLY TO ME.

For my salvation
Free me from damnation
Also free from maddening wrath
Of fathers, lovers and children.

To make me fit for the world
To mould me into what already is
To start with a new understanding
In the arms that held me close.

I nodded in assent
Accepting every word in truest spirit
Straining every cell in my body to limit
End the breathless search for the exit.

WORDS ON A HIGHWAY

Headed for a highway thrill
Of a sudden caught, in the middle
Look, here is no right or left
My own lights will this story tell.

Is there room for genuine strife
When no mistakes allowed in life?
I drive my own dreams
I make my own talk with fortis.

Thoughts stop for an instant
Before the mind goes still;
My car is on continuous course
A taste of life-blood which is indispensible.

What trickery is built into our structures
That separate ever and ever me from others?
Friendship cries to cross tougher barriers
As my road of no remorse extends further.

DURGA

Tomorrow yet she will come
Every year to every home
Warm each hearth in brief spurt.

The merriment is without restraint
She has returned to her form quaint
Not just worshipped as goddess or saint.

She is the embodiment of their culture
Like them she has family structure
To be escorted in this life and life in future.

A daughter of great beauty
A wife companion worthy
In all she leaves her identity.